FAN[illegible]
BE[illegible]
AND WHERE
TO FIND THEM

FANTASTIC BEINGS AND WHERE TO FIND THEM

HOW TO CONTACT SPACE ALIENS, INTELLIGENCES, AND PEOPLE

VALIANT THOR

FANTASTIC BEINGS AND WHERE TO FIND THEM

ISBN-13: 978-1530932054
ISBN-10: 153093205X

PRINTING HISTORY
Galaxy Press edition published 1960
Saucerian Press edition published 1973
New Age Press edition published 1984
New Saucerian Press edition published 2016

FOREWORD

How to Contact Space Aliens was narrated by the great Venusian teacher, Valiant Thor, at our humble request. This transcription is intended especially for you, the New Age individual, to uplift and guide you on the path of higher contact.

The complete technique by which you may reach the high consciousness of interplanetary beings and contact them, is revealed for the first time in this book. (Our Venusian brothers considered it unwise to reveal certain details of higher contact before we were ready.)

This book contains some of the best information I have been privileged to pass along. It also brings you the latest, up-to-the-minute ideas, conclusions, and instructions for your important New Age work in the service of others.

A new phase of the Great Plan is now under way. Activity on the flying saucer horizon has not ended. It is just beginning! Our space brothers now wish to make conscious contact, through special Thought Transmission, with many thousands more of us New Age individuals on planet Earth.

Your important part in this wonderful New Age activity is outlined herein. You are about to open a door into a fabulous universe. Proceed carefully and cautiously, following instructions closely. Do not try to rush things. Allow yourself time to unfold this new and wonderful experience.

-Michael X. Barton

CHAPTER 1

SOUL CONTACT: VENUSIAN STYLE

SOUL CONTACT is the most important thing we could possibly do at this time for ourselves and for others. This is so vitally important now. Why? Because the Higher Self intelligence of each individual is his or her best teacher and guide.

Your soul is able to communicate with the Higher Self, and carry on a two-way conversation with it. Thus will you receive the most valuable higher wisdom and guidance. For it is the still, small voice speaking within you that can guide and direct you clearly in the way you should go as you travel THE PATH.

With such divine guidance (for it is actually the voice of God speaking to you), darkness and confusion is dispelled and you move swiftly on the true path of LIGHT.

At this time, as the Old Piscean Age is rapidly drawing to a dramatic ending, walking with those in the Light is important. Walking in the Path of Light is very important. And walking in the Path of Love is MOST important!

Love is the Key to reaching up into the Higher Consciousness. Yes, it is a fact. Higher Contact is made only by those who love, for love lifts us into a very high awareness.

Many New Age Individuals are sending a great vibration of pure love out to other human beings at this time. This is most helpful, for as we realize, the "Sifting" of human souls is now going on. During this Sifting period, we must try to help others come up into a higher state of awareness.

Only a very few of them will understand and respond. "Mass-minded" men and women will not understand what is going on right under their very eyes. But you and all other New Age Souls shall understand. You shall keep faith with your teachers and with your higher self.

Mass-programmed "Normals" will continue moving in circles, because they are dependent on physical, material senses only. They must see, hear, touch, smell, and taste in order to believe. Unhappily, such persons are "trapped" in matter. They lack inner vision to see the spiritual realities that exist behind material things.

But do not feel undue concern over those souls. No soul is ever lost in the Great Plan. Laggard souls are simply "harvested" by the Etheric Beings in charge of such things, and taken to a less-evolved planet in another solar system, where conditions are more in keeping with their stubborn nature.

You, the New Age Individual, by your study and practice of these higher teachings, are spiraling up beyond the "trap" of dense matter and its limitations. You are moving upward into a faster vibration, where the Light from your Higher Self can pour through you in ever-increasing radiance.

Soul Contact is the next step to take. And the magic of higher contact is simply this: Before seeking to contact the Saucer Beings, we are to make genuine contact with our own Soul. Via the Soul, we reach upward to make further contacts. Having done that, other contacts with Saucer Beings will follow in a natural, easy sequence.

Each of you has a most wonderful opportunity now to become a more perfect and useful "channel" for the Light, and a marvelous "receiver" of higher communications. According to your sincere desire to be of service to the "Brothers of the Higher Arc," you will you become a living center of Life, Love, and Wisdom.

In this regard, I must speak of the Subliminal State of mind. It has an important relationship to higher contact. The Subliminal State is a condition of "Conscious plus Subconscious awareness." When you acquire the art of relaxing your physical body completely, you find that your mind gains greater freedom.

Although your conscious mind is fairly inactive, your deeper mind, the subconscious, is most active. Gradually, it begins to function throughout the entire brain. You are no longer hampered by little hindrances, and soon experience HEIGHTENED AWARENESS.

Edgar Cayce, the seer of Virginia Beach, became quite proficient at entering into the "Subliminal State" of mind. That state led him gently into the higher, or "Superconscious State" of mind. Wisdom then poured through him, and he was enabled to assist many thousands of sincere individuals, by giving them psychic readings as to the real nature of their physical ills and the best means of treatment.

In my book "Venusian Secret Science," the complete technique of getting into the subliminal state is presented in easy-to-understand, step-by-step procedure. Those who haven't yet learned this important technique, which is very basic to any contact with the higher forces, should secure this valuable information as soon as possible.

Now, we come to a very interesting subject: Definitions. How do we define "Space People?" For some time now, many of us have used the term "Space People" or "Space Beings" in referring to all beings who travel in flying saucers and various types of spacecraft. This is true; these are "Space People," defined as those who are able to travel safely in outer space.

The fact is, however, that there are many different kinds of beings who inhabit space.

Human beings, for example, who have attained mastership over matter by working knowingly with Light (and that includes mastery of their finer bodies), are able to lay aside the heavy material body and travel in a mental body. They can then move with the speed of thought. All space is their home, and they do not require physical or etheric spacecraft in order to navigate anywhere in our solar system. Can we not also call these astral bodies "Space People?"

There are also Etheric Beings. These are human dwellers on the various etheric planes in the universe. They live in worlds just as real to them as ours is to us, but they have no dense material flesh body as we do. These, too, are Space People.

There are also the WATCHERS. In the Holy Bible, they are called "watchers from a far country." They are physical human beings very similar to us, but whose home is not on Earth. In order to reach your planet, they use spacecraft capable of interplanetary flight. Although they have physical bodies, they are of a much higher vibratory frequency than most Earth bodies, and are far more "etherealized."

Most of these Watchers come from the more highly evolved planets such as Venus, Mars, and others. They have been observing your planet intently since 1947. They are aware of the critical condition your planet is in, now that it has the secret of atomic power. Atomic radiation due to the many atom bomb tests has caused more havoc than most of us realize. But that is not all.

We now live in a cosmic time. Our entire solar system is entering a new and higher region of light. Changes of a cosmic nature are definitely due for this planet and for us.

In the days of Noah, people were told to "flee to the high mountains." Now we are not told to flee to the mountains, but rather to "stand in the Holy Place."

Where is the Holy Place? It is within you. It is the sacred shrine that each individual now must build within himself. For within that shrine shall come the "telepathic call," the guidance from your own Higher Self Intelligence.

Divine direction will come. Your responsibility and mine is to diligently train ourselves to be better "receiving sets" for higher thoughts and impressions. In ancient times, the word given Ezekiel was: "Behold, Son of Man, I set thee a Watchman to warn my people."

Yes, the Watchman will warn us at the proper time. But it will be an inner warning, an inner voice rather than an outer voice. And it will come through the mechanism of your own awakened Soul.

We said that these are conclusive days. Magnificently big changes are impending. The Brothers of the "Higher Arc" are far more aware of the nature of these changes than you are. That is why many noble beings from extremely high and spiritual realms are coming to your planet, and why they have been observing your world for so long. They desire to be near this Earth, to better assist you in these conclusive days.

And here is a most important point: These High Brothers I now refer to are Etheric Beings.

But they come from an etheric level infinitely higher and more refined than any of those surrounding this planet. Their order of intelligence is far greater and far more spiritual than anything known to us.

These wonderful beings have made the great sacrifice of taking on an etheric body much denser than the fine spiritual bodies they normally wear. They themselves do not call this a sacrifice. They use denser bodies to be near us at this time. It is not easy for them to be in Earth's lower vibrations, but as it is necessary for you to be guided, they have come.

They are near us, guiding us, leading us. Why? To enable all sincere souls to perfect themselves and enlighten others. As we do this, we shall realize what Saint Paul was speaking of when he said: "And we will be caught up into the air to meet Him." This event is the "Great Airlift" spoken of in the Bible and other sacred books.

If you put forth the sustained effort that is required to reach higher consciousness, I assure you that you SHALL make the grade! Your spiritual light will begin to shine with ever-increasing brightness. THAT bright light will positively attract the attention of the "Brothers of the Higher Arc."

They will see your light and draw closer to you. Then higher contact will become a reality to you – a glorious, living reality. YOU WILL THEN BE A "CONTACTEE," and all your doubts will be gone.

The Brothers, of course, become interested in you only when they observe that your light is shining brightly. For they know that you are then READY to contact them, and that your motive is pure and that you are reaching upward to them for GREATER LIGHT. Believe me, they are happy to receive you!

Remember, however, that it is far more important for each of us to find the "voice of God" within us, and be guided by that voice than to depend upon any other person or persons. In our upward journey into LIGHT, LOVE, and LIBERATION, we are assigned higher Teachers to assist us. Their duty is to aid us in making our own inner connection with the "Diamond Star" – the Soul-Center within our own hearts.

So never lose sight of that purpose. You will enjoy the loving companionship of many wise and noble teachers as you travel the UPWARD PATH. They will imbue you with a zeal, fervor, and enthusiasm you've never before experienced! You will thrill with joy and gratitude, for their light will enable you to carry out your particular job at this time and in the days to come. I tell you it will be THRILLING!

Light is now increasing, for our sun system is entering new regions of light. People everywhere on the planet are starting to wake up to a new STIMULUS. Some understand it; others are still in the "dark" as to its source and meaning.

The amazing fact is that our entire solar system is moving into new and powerful regions of light in God's universe. It is the sign that we are nearing the close of the Old Dispensation and stepping boldly into the NEW ERA. As we do so, the intensity of cosmic light energy is being increased to such a degree that those who are on the side of LIGHT will express constantly greater light and "inner knowing."

In fact, sincere New Age souls will SHINE with light, so that their very bodies and garments will radiate MORE LIGHT. They will symbolize uplift. This is the time of cosmic light, when great light shall beam from all of us! The dark karmic history of Europe will recede into the past.

Our friend Edgar Cayce gave one of his remarkable psychic readings in 1934, in which he said: "The upper portion of Europe will be CHANGED in the twinkling of an eye."

As the great light gradually increases, there is greater contrast between those "in the light" and those enmeshed in materiality. So do not be alarmed if you are misunderstood by the multitudes (and your relatives). They have not awakened.

We are aware, you and I, that NOW is the time for a great INWARD PREPARATION. That is why we have been gathered together with one united purpose: to CONTACT THE LIGHT – to get ourselves attuned, so that we are enabled to know and commune with the guiding minds of spiritually advanced teachers.

We live in a great time. There is a great and glorious destiny just ahead for all true New Age individuals. We are going to realize that glorious destiny. The Sons and Daughters of Light, in one strong and united body, are moving onward, upward, and Godward. And as we move upward under the higher direction of the Brothers and our own Higher Self intelligence, we become mighty torches of assistance!

Your flame will become so bright that it will enlighten and assist countless numbers of "New Age Souls," who are only waiting for your light to uplift them. But it is also your divine responsibility, as a New Age Individual, to maintain inner poise and control in all of the higher activities you engage in. Poise, control, and balance must be your guideposts.

Find your own center of Christ Balance, and then reach upward to commune with the higher beings. Express love from your Soul Center. This will keep you balanced and harmonious at all times.

Guard against emotional imbalance, for over-excitability hinders clear thinking. Develop a deep inner calm and peace, for that is your assurance of protection from the Wise Ones.

Walk this Path, reach UPWARD in thought and love, and you, too, will know the MAGIC of higher contact. With this wisdom, the Powers of Light will walk with you.

CHAPTER 2

HOW TO UPLIFT

We Venusians say that Higher Love is the keynote of the coming New Age. Why? Because Higher Love seeks balance, and balance is the great secret of Harmony, Peace, Health, and all Wisdom. This higher love is different from Earthly love.

Earthly love is important, but it so often binds us instead of releasing us into greater freedom. The reason it does so is because it generally lacks the "balance" factor, and is based more upon receiving than giving.

Higher love frees, releases, and harmonizes everything it contacts. It is not possessive or restrictive. Rather, it brings you a realization of "oneness" and a joyous, harmonious freedom that makes your heart sing in gratitude. When you come into this happy feeling, it is like warm sunshine beaming down upon you from above. You feel its gentle rays and want to bask in that sunshine of Higher Love forever.

When you come to an understanding of this higher love, to the point where you desire harmony, health, and happiness with all creation, then you will be ready to reach out to Venus and other worlds, and extend the hand of love to them. The Lord Thinkers of Venus will then welcome and embrace you openly.

But you know as well as I do that the highly spiritualized minds on advanced planets are not going to stand for any childish attempts by Earthmen to "conquer" outer space through brute force. No indeed.

The Lords and Teachers of Venus are very wise. War and violence have long since been banished from our glorious world. It is the planet of the Christ-Love principle, and we intend to keep it that way. Gently but firmly, we convey a realization of higher love, and this love is essential before the "astronauts" of Earth will really master interplanetary flight. Until you are willing to extend a hand of love, you shall continue to "miss your target," time after time.

The first requisite is to practice giving freely of your higher love vibration. When you desire within your heart, mind, and soul to harmonize, unify, and uplift any person or situation, you are sending out the right vibration. It is a desire or yearning for a condition of exquisite harmony, wellbeing, and happiness to exist within all living beings. This is higher love. Give freely of it.

Expand your love to take in all races all men, women, and children on all planets as one great brotherhood. Then we shall all be working together in harmony for the unlimited GOOD of all humanity. As we New Age souls express more love for others, all men and nature will work together joyously in Cooperative Brotherhood.

This is the way of love. It is the way to uplift others now.

Are you often greatly puzzled as to how you may best assist your friends and loved ones who do not realize these New Age Truths the way you do? Here is the answer. You CAN uplift them into a new, higher and happier vibration by doing THREE things for them:

1. Bless them by recognizing that each soul is a center of Light, Love, and Life. Mentally project to them an image of themselves as being lifted into a new vibration, wherein they see the "Shining Presence" of their own beautiful Higher

Self.

2. Send the clear thought of Peace and Goodwill to those persons you wish to assist. Mentally "spray" their auras with uplifting, pacifying thoughts of peace on Earth, Goodwill to all living beings.

3. Send living energies of color by visualizing these from yourself to those you would help. Colors of the light pink, green, blue, violet, etc. are powerful soul-energizers. Each color has a specific energizing or releasing effect.

These three simple things will make a definite, constructive change in anybody. Not only do the sender and receiver benefit, but also the good vibrations go out to uplift, harmonize, and add joy to the entire planet. This will assist all other New Age individuals to make higher contact with the loving souls of Venus. And it will assist you to make contact also, for harmony and balance are the keys to all higher communications.

The more who follow these guidelines, the greater the uplift. We do not have to use our mental or will-force to tell a person to "do this" or "do that," but just simply send out to them the positive vibrations of Peace and Love. And bless that person, so he will become aware of his True Self and awaken into a new and wonderful consciousness.

The Space People have clever ways of illustrating their ideas. In school on Venus, they would show us a picture of a large block of ice, in which a fish had been frozen. Nearby was a large axe. Now, how could I release that fish from his prison of ice? My first thought was to grab the axe and chop into the block of ice.

"That would be like imposing your will," said my Venusian mentor. "But what would happen? The axe might cut into the ice so deeply and sharply that the fish would be injured or killed."

Then the answer to the problem was presented. All that we needed to do was to place the block of frozen ice out in the direct sunlight. The sun's warm rays melted the ice and freed the captive fish. No force or violence was required.

To release any person from some negative condition, all you need to do is remember that little lesson of how the fish was freed from its state of suspension. Souls too, get suspended in low vibrations, and in discord and illness. They are in a sense frozen in ice, like the fish. While in that negative condition of suspension, they cannot make progress. But you and I can help by sending them love. Love melts the ice.

When the ice melts, the soul unfolds and awakens of its own accord. On your planet, we are to help one another unfold, and the finest way to do that is by sending out the vibration of love in the color essence of rosy, radiant pink. Tincture the color well with golden light.

Pink assists in bringing about a state of wellbeing and optimism to others. It lifts them up. They begin to see life through "rose-colored glasses" as it were, and this is wonderful, for it sets them free of discordant thoughts.

In sending out this cosmic love vibration, visualize a pure white light pouring down into you from above. See it entering through the top of your head and filling your heart with a golden white radiance. Now visualize that golden white radiance in your heart turning into a golden pink.

As soon as you become aware of the pink color, send it out with full power to those you wish to help. Send it out from your heart center to theirs. See the pink color going out from you and wrapping itself as a radiant mantle around the heart center of others, awakening them into a joyous new freedom. This will release them into harmony that will permeate their words and acts.

By sending the higher love vibration of this golden pink light to your friends and loved ones, you will be doing them a tremendous service. This will help wipe away a great deal of bad Karma you may have accrued through your own past incarnations on this planet.

And though you may not at once notice the difference in the appearance or actions of the ones you have thus helped, have patience. We have seen this technique succeed time and time again across the galaxy, leading to the spiritual ascension of many.

CHAPTER 3

WILL YOU BE A CONTACTEE?

The answer to this important question is YES. I am quite certain that if you choose to be a Contactee, you will become one. How soon depends upon your sincerity and faithfulness.

We Space Brothers desire to make conscious contact with more and more individuals in all walks of life. The reason we desire this is because we have a Great Plan that we are serving, which is powerful, cosmic, and universal in scope.

That Plan is simple in essence, but complex and intricate in its ramifications. The average Earth-man's mind is not "geared up" to grasp this Cosmic Plan, because he has not advanced to this higher octave of being that the Space Brothers and Sisters have realized. It is wonderful that they have an earnest desire to contact more and more of the New Age souls that are now awakened.

Now, at the present time on this planet, there are

already more than 100,000 awakened souls. The goal is a minimum of from six to ten million who are fully aware of their presence and purpose here. Since 1944 (three years prior to Kenneth Arnold's sighting) the Brothers of the Higher Arc have come into your atmosphere, to fulfill a 100-year plan in the higher interests of Earth and its people.

With great caution and wisdom, the Brothers did not reveal to any one individual the entire workings of the Plan. One by one, they have been contacting the "awakened ones" of Earth, and teaching them a certain part of this wonderful plan.

Bit by bit, the pieces have been gathered together, and we are letting you see the great overall picture much more clearly. Not even the Contactees knew the vast scope of this Great Plan, but at least the complete picture is being filled in.

The Plan is so big that it requires a great dedication of each New Age soul to tell others, so that we can uplift more of humanity into a new octave of vibration. That is the goal. You will find a few clues in your seventh chapter of the Book of Revelation. And if you think there are only 144,000 "saved" souls, read the second half of that chapter.

The Creator has a mighty Plan. The Higher Brothers are consciously cooperating with that Plan, just as you will when you become more aware of it. The Plan includes not only your planet Earth, but also all of the planets in our solar system.

It is an uplift in the vibratory frequency of this entire solar system. It is a cosmic upgrading of the planets and their inhabitants. And although the big change may come suddenly, nature is leading up to it very gradually, just as she does in all her work. There is a period of growth and preparation, and then, finally, the "fruition." We are now approaching that time of fruition.

That is why souls on Earth are awakening now. Never before in history have more people begun to LOOK UP to the wise beings from other worlds for guidance and instruction. You realize that something BIG is impending, something of COSMIC MAGNITUDE. Something that touches each and every one of us deeply, whether the laggard souls accept it or not.

That's why you yearn for Higher Contact. You are seeking actual connection and attunement with the Creator's Plan. You wish to align yourself with that Great Plan and with the Higher Brothers, because they are themselves aligned with it.

The way is simple, easy, and painless. It is simply a beautiful blending of the principles of Intelligence,

Love, and Power in beautiful harmony. This is the real key to Higher Contact. You are stepping up into a wonderful new vibration – a higher dimensional state. This dimension will thrill you to the very depths of your soul when you attune harmoniously.

Each awakened soul has a special role to play in this mighty New Age drama. It is principally the job of awakening and harmonizing other souls. But no two of us will serve in the same capacity. Each will have his or her own unique manner of serving the bigger Plan, so there will be practically no duplication of roles.

As more of us find our place in this activity (and no New Age individual is happy until he does), we will start to raise the "mass consciousness" in a wonderful way. The awareness of the masses of people on this planet will be stepped up.

You will not ALL be awakened, but millions of you will be. Millions will be "Contactees" by the end of the century. You very likely shall be one of these loving, enlightened brothers and sisters. You'll be centered and poised in the mightiest principle – that of BALANCED LIGHT. This is the beautiful balance of Love, Power, and Wisdom within you.

Are you ready for Higher Contact? If you are

certain that your motive for contacting the Space Brothers is pure, then the answer is "yes." Purity of motive is most important; this means simply that you are not seeking to contact the Brothers merely to satisfy curiosity.

Curiosity-seekers are often selfish souls who are more interested in their own petty desires than in serving the Great Plan. Any self-seeking motive keeps one's soul-vibration at too low an octave of vibration. This hinders all higher communications.

Therefore, clarify your real motive first. With purity of motive (serving the highest Universal Will and Purpose), you then should devote 5 minutes in the morning, 5 minutes at noon, and 5 minutes at night to conscious recognition of your own "X" or Higher Self. The Higher Self dwells on a plane above your human personality, and is always attuned to the CHRIST-BALANCED LIGHT in the universe.

And here is the SECRET. The more of that BALANCED LIGHT you receive from your Higher Self, the more perfectly balanced you will be in body, mind, and soul. With balance you are much better able to carry on an intelligent and rational conversation with Space People, who are highly advanced mentally and spiritually.

Call for the BALANCED LIGHT every time you think of your Higher Self. Ask that the light be sent down into your brain and heart chakras. This marvelous practice clears your mental channels for telepathic communications from us.

We do want each and every one of you to be a Contactee, and we are confident that you can become one. It is high time that Earthmen awaken from their dreams and connect to REALITY.

The Christ Light is tremendously real. We Space Brothers and Sisters are real, and so are our celestial ships. A Contactee must anchor himself to reality at all costs. Following the siren call of fantasy, imagination, and make-believe will only result in self-delusion and imbalance. Before you reach for contact, you must seek first the Balanced Light.

Invoke thought communications with Higher Beings, and practice harmony and poise. Balance, success, love, and happiness will follow.

Becoming a Contactee is your New Age privilege. Now is the time to apply the secrets given you for your higher progress.

If you invoke the Light as directed, and use great zeal in carrying out instructions, you WILL become a Contactee.

CHAPTER 4

VALIANT THOR NEEDS YOU NOW!

Yes, a totally new and marvelous phase of the Great Plan is now beginning to unfold. It is WORLD LIBERATION. It is the second act in the mighty drama that involves every one of us. You are needed to assist the Space People in liberating mankind from its hopeless burden of negative "Karma."

Here is what we desire you to do now.

Condition yourself now for conscious contact, mind-to-mind, with we Venusians and other Brothers of the Higher Arc. Do this by purifying your MOTIVES first of all.

Purity of motive is the GREAT SECRET of making Higher Contact. And the purest motive is simply this: To follow in perfect accord with the Plan of that Great Being we call our Creator.

Do not listen to false prophets who preach hatred and division. They will often come in a suit and tie, telling you that they are going to solve all your problems, and "Make America Great Again." These wolves in sheep's clothing cannot be trusted, and often secretly work for your enemies.

Play the Creator's trump card, which is love, solid reasoning, and transparency. God has it all figured out. Jesus never preached hatred, racism, or misogyny. His Plan comes down from high spiritual sources through the great Balanced Light. It is the purest Light known, and it shines on people of all races, creeds, and colors.

As your innermost motive attunes with the motive of the Creator, your light expands, and as it expands, the Space Brothers become aware of it, and will come to assist you.

At first, we will guide you gently, without your knowing it, perhaps. Later, as you grow stronger and more valuable to the cause, you will be contacted telepathically, and will receive instruction and "working orders" directly from Space Brothers like myself.

Of your own free choice (never because of what I or anyone else says), begin to adopt a more vital, natural, and organic diet. How and what you eat will affect your ability to "tune-in" with the Space Brothers. You can raise or lower your personal vibrations by the kinds of food you put into your stomach. The eating of processed or genetically modified foods causes a dark shadow or cloud to form upon the etheric body.

The etheric body is the pattern or sustaining "vehicle" upon which the physical body is built. A person with clairvoyant vision can at one once perceive the dark cloud that forms on the inner body when one eats processed foods.

This cloud acts as an interference or obstruction to the Balanced Light that is sent down from the Higher Self. Unless the light from your Higher Self can get through easily, your vibration remains too low in intensity for clear and easy communication with the minds of the Space People.

As you gradually make the required change in your diet and open yourself to the inflow of Ascension Light, the cloud that may now be obstructing your higher contact will start to dissolve. When we begin to embrace the Great Purpose of the Guiding Mind that brought us into being and that directs the cosmos, the conflicts and cognitive dissonance within us dissolve.

You will find that if you make the effort to set aside your ego and reach up for the greater Light, Love, and Power coming now from the Creator, an amazing thing will happen. The Space Brothers will help you to "connect up" with the Light of your Higher Self. It will then become easier and easier for you to set aside your petty desires for something far, far grander and nobler. You will find one day that the selfish ego has "melted" or submerged itself into the Greater Will.

Then, as more Light pours into your brain and higher centers (pituitary and pineal glands), you will notice a wonderful new mental clarity. The thoughts of the highly intelligent beings of Venus and other advanced worlds will then come into your consciousness clearly.

When your light shines brighter, you will be *seen* by the "Brothers of the Higher Arc." One of them, your present teacher on your own individual wavelength, will get in touch with you telepathically. This will happen only at the proper time. When it occurs, do not be startled or alarmed. It is most important for you to observe the following practice.

Obtain for yourself at least one or two psychic gems or stones. You will use them to raise your vibrations, to enable you to project your thoughts and commune with us.

It is essential that all psychic gems be first "purified"

of any mixed magnetisms (of low vibration) and then spiritually "charged" with the high potency light from the Higher Self. The crystal or psychic stone then becomes imbued with the Balanced Light vibration of the spiritual self.

This is a powerful aid to contacting us, since the "charged" stone steps up your capacity to receive as well as transmit thoughts. All that is necessary is to place the charged stone upon your head so that it is directly over your pituitary gland. Unless a psychic stone is properly demagnetized and charged with the Light power from the Higher Self, it is not fully effective for Higher Contact. (See *Venusian Secret Science* for more details.)

Set aside a regular time for Higher Communication. It is preferable to have this contact just after you rise in the morning, but before breakfast. It should always be at the same time each day, and in the same room.

Now, at the exact time you have chosen, sit down at your desk or table with pen and pad ready. Hold your pen so that only the point is lightly touching the paper.

Your objective is to contact your Cosmic Teacher mentally during the next 15 minutes. When contact is made, he will use your arm to write his name first. (Let the pen move freely of its own accord. You may sense a kind of electric impulse prompting movement in your arm.)

If the name is slow in coming, mentally request your Cosmic Teacher to give you the name he wishes to be known by. He will do so if you have qualified for communication with him, by the new brightness of your own light.

And he may also identify himself to you by means of a special symbol uniquely his own. For example, I often identify myself to Earthlings through the sign of the Golden Ram. With the sign comes an individual vibration that no other being can duplicate, for no two beings have the same vibration. (All of us are individuals with different soul and spirit patterns.)

Your teacher will identify himself clearly and positively at the first successful Contact Time. At the end of your contact, say that you are ready to discontinue if agreeable with the Teacher. Wait until he signs off, by giving his name, before you leave. This "sign-off" procedure is important and must not be neglected. It insures against the possible entrance of lower astral entities (elementals) at this vulnerable point.

We are not endorsing "automatic writing" as such,

and later on, your teacher may not need to write through your hand. You will know when to discontinue the writing, because you will begin to get more and more of your teacher's inspirational words or ideas. You may even begin to receive "picture thoughts" that you will be able to recognize as coming from your Teacher.

But you will use your regular time for Higher Communication. And you may continue using the psychic stone or other psychic aids. When using the stone, do not try to hold the stone in place with your hand. Either "tape" it to your forehead, between the eyes, or place it on top of the head, using a lightweight hat to keep it in place while you are concentrating on the communication.

Next, mentally surround yourself with a golden white light. Visualize it pouring down from above into your entire body and immersing you in a great Tube of Light. This is your protection against undesired low vibrations. As you gaze quietly at the pure white light, soon the muscles of your eyes will relax slightly.

You are inducing a condition known as the Subliminal State of awareness. In this condition, you will become more sensitive to the thought energies of the Space Brothers.

All physical aids can be dispensed with later, but not until your "attunement" has been well established.

After gazing quietly at the Tube of Light for five minutes, slowly count to seven. With each count, mentally request your consciousness to rise higher and higher. Without this "steppingstone" stepping-up process, mental contact is much more difficult to achieve. After mental contact has been achieved and the teacher has "signed off" by giving his name, begin counting, IN REVERSE, from seven back down to ONE, slowly.

Then with open eyes, stamp your foot once on the floor to assert symbolically that you have returned to your normal state of consciousness. Under no circumstances should you neglect this!

These are the secret techniques you have been waiting for. Put them to work for you at once. Do not feel discouraged if you fail to make contact immediately. It merely means that you must continue invoking the Light and raising your body vibrations.

Practice makes perfect. Like any other reward in life, Higher Contact must be earned. THOUGHT, FEELING, and ACTION, working together harmoniously and in balance at the highest level, will prepare you for this great experience.

I urge you to reach up now, for the Higher Brothers are calling you.

CHAPTER 5

COSMIC FAQ (FREQUENTLY ASKED QUESTIONS)

How soon will I be contacted by the Saucer People?

This depends upon you. We Space Brothers are making mental contacts now with those individuals who are more advanced than the majority of the people. You can earn your contact by following directions carefully. In time, ALL New Age individuals will be contacted.

Is two-way telepathic communication with intelligent interplanetary beings possible?

Not only is it possible, but "Contactees" in all parts of the world are doing it. At present time, most of this communication is done at a relatively short distance between the spacecraft in your atmosphere and you.

What are the benefits of contact with Space People?

Tremendous new mind and soul freedom through contact with powerful and advanced intelligences – beings who have actually connected up with universal reality.

Can every sincere individual become a Contactee?

Sincerity is very important. However, purity of one's motive is the biggest determining factor. We Space Brothers can only accomplish our good purpose by carefully choosing those who are mature enough to be loyal and dedicated cooperators in the Great Plan.

Will my Space Teacher communicate with me in English?

He will communicate in whatever language is most familiar to you.

Are there many different types of Space People?

Yes, there are 1) Physical beings whose vibratory frequency is considerably higher than yours; 2) Etheric beings who dwell in the etheric regions around the earth and around other planets; and 3) Celestial beings involved in the causation of creation (angelic beings). The first two classifications are made up of our Elder Brothers and Sisters who have already advanced to the next "Higher Arc" of soul, mind, and body. They make use of Spaceships, Space Stations, and mental contact methods.

Does life on Venus resemble our life on Earth?

Yes, but it is more spiritual. Our underground installations prevent certain physical activities, but this is more than made up for with psychic and mental activities, which can be quite glorious.

How may I be sure it is really my Space Teacher who is in contact with me telepathically, and not my own mind speaking to me?

First, you will notice a rapid delivery of ideas to you when a Brother of the Higher Arc is in contact with you. Your own mind is not generally as definitive and swift in its functioning. Second, the knowledge your Space Teacher gives you will be completely unlike anything you are now aware of.

How can I protect myself against beings from the lower astral planes?

Like attracts like in the mental realms. If you keep your physical, mental, and soul vibrations high through higher thought, higher feelings, and higher deeds, your aura and mental wavelength instantly repel the lower elementals. It is up to you whom you will commune with, just as it is up to you to make the decision as to which friends you prefer. Purity of motive protects you best, because it permits more powerful Light from the Higher Self to flow into your body. Lower entities cannot tolerate the higher vibration of that Light.

Why are the Space Brothers contacting us?

For World Liberation. We are cleaning the astral realms inside and outside of Earth, and freeing your minds of "Old World" concepts. This new and higher phase of our work is about contacting as many humans as possible, with the purpose of preparing this planet and your people for the coming "Initiation in Light."

Why is it that good has had such little effect on the bad in our world? Why is there so much wrong on Earth?

Because Earth people, generally speaking, have not yet accepted the Christlike, balanced way of life. Man does not consciously recognize the importance of keeping harmony with all of nature. His own soul is asleep to the universal realities of limitless LIFE, LOVE, and LIGHT all around and within himself. Simply put, Man has ignored the God-Plan of Higher Love. In its place, you have substituted egoism, to dominate and conquer all creation by mental cunning and sheer physical might. Most human leaders see only the outer, material appearances of things. Only a small number see the soul within all things.

Is Venus really inhabited by human beings?

YES. This is so. Venus is inhabited by advanced souls. It is the home of joyous students leading an exalted human life. Jesus lived on Venus before his birth on planet Earth. Those on Venus have physical bodies, but of a much higher vibratory frequency than yours, and they radiate more Light at all times.

Who will go to Venus?

Venus is the planet of Divine Christlike Love. Only a handful of Earth's humanity have awakened to this high vibration of perfect love. Only the more spiritual and selfless souls of Earth are ready for Venusian life – those who are now actively developing an awareness of higher love, harmony vibration, beauty, and oneness.

Do certain stones or psychic gems make contact easier?

Yes. Edgar Cayce recommended the Lapis Lingua

stone, while Rudolf Steiner recommends the quartz crystal – the basis for the computer chip (which stores information). On Venus, we prefer the boron crystal, which can easily be found on Earth. Remember, properly "charging" any psychic stone requires that the person charging the stone be able to invoke a spiritual Light Power from his higher self and infuse it into the stone. This does require a definite ritual, as well as the authentic desire to invoke higher spiritual energy for purposes of good.

Where is the best place to find an alien to communicate with?

The location does not matter. You will be found by us based on your vibratory wavelength. You could be in a cave or underground bunker, and we would still be able to find you.

Can your provide any tips for charging a psychic stone?

Here are some step-by-step instructions. They are not complicated or hard to follow, but each step is important.

Because any stone has mixed vibrations and may have passed through many hands before you obtained it, you must first demagnetize it, so as to banish all traces of past vibratory influences.

Take the gem up in your hands so that the fingers and thumb of your left hand hold one end of the stone, while the fingers and thumb of your right hand hold the other end of the stone. Now hold the stone quietly and think strongly of your highest ideal of LIFE, LOVE, and LIGHT, for five to ten minutes. This "demagnetizes" the stone of all lower vibrations.

After you have done this, set the stone down on a table and DO NOT TOUCH IT for ten full minutes. Above all, do not allow anyone else handle the stone. At the end of ten minutes, pick up the stone again, hold it as you did before in both hands, and breathe on it slowly.

As you breathe, inject the full intensity of your mind and thought upon the stone, seeing in your "mind's eye" the words LIFE, LOVE, and LIGHT as if they were being written, engraved, or impressed on the stone. Do this for a full five minutes.

The stone is now charged with your own personal and highest vibrations. From now on, allow no one but yourself to handle it, for strange magnetism will affect it negatively.

The stone is now ready for use in assisting you to raise and intensify your mental vibrations so that thought communication with the Space People will be possible.

Invoking or calling us is the next phase of this higher work. Invocation serves two purposes. First, it will attune you with our higher consciousness. Secondly, it will help the world in general.

It is unwise to petition higher beings for merely selfish or material reasons. Requests should be only in regard to spiritual matters, such as will advance the world spiritually.

Also, an Invocation should never be made kneeling down, for the act of kneeling down lowers your whole vibratory consciousness, and may bring you into attunement with the lower worlds of beings. This is never desirable. The aerial spaces are thronged with countless intelligences, some good, pure, true, and celestial. Others are just the opposite.

To reach the true and good ones, such as the high beings of Venus, your heart must correspond by invoking only the good, true, and beautiful for noble purposes. Therefore it is best to stand upright, holding the psychic stone in your right hand, so it rests lightly in your open palm.

Now, LOOK UP and address the Space Beings silently and mentally.

Do not speak aloud, for the spoken word is too Earth-bound. Think from within, upwards, and always silently. Remember, we Space Beings are master telepathists. And we are looking for the aid of sincere Earthlings. Here is the Invocation you should use to contact a Spacemaster:

> Oh Cosmic Teacher of LIFE, LOVE, and LIGHT from the planet Venus, may the Spirit of Goodness manifest on this Earth as it does on Venus.
>
> May the positive powers of LIFE, LOVE, and LIGHT overcome all negation and usher in the NEW and GOLDEN AGE.
>
> Through the magic of mind, reach out to me now, that my soul may increase in Cosmic Wisdom and Love for the GOOD of all Life, and the glory of the Great Creator.

Now you are prepared mentally and spiritually for CONCENTRATION.

Here is a method my Contactees personally use when they want to RECEIVE a message from outer space. They hold the psychic stone to their forehead, just above and between their eyes. (This place is directly in front of the pineal gland, the psychic organ of telepathic reception.)

By exerting a moderate, firm pressure over this area, you will find that the vibrations of the stone act to "step up" the vibrations of your thoughts, thus aiding your ability to CONCENTRATE mentally on outer space communications.

Whenever you wish to TRANSMIT or send a mental message to your Spacemaster, raise the stone to the top or crown of your head, and hold it there while exerting moderately firm pressure. (This spot is directly above the pineal gland.)

By applying gentle pressure to the stone at this spot just over the "third-eye," you will find that the vibrations of the stone aid greatly in focusing and intensifying your thought-force, so that you can transmit your own thoughts more positively and with a higher degree of success.

Another method we use is called the "Awareness Slide." Here you visualize the spectrum between your own conscious and subconscious thoughts as a string. And on that string, you mentally imagine placing your finger, and moving your finger toward the subconscious end of the spectrum. This will allow more and more of your unconscious and subconscious thoughts to rise to conscious awareness, thus aiding your ability to send and receive telepathic signals.

The Venusians embody love and wisdom. If you will seek to emulate those virtues and embody them in your soul and personality, you will find that after a while, you will bring yourself into that state where you naturally create an AFFINITY between yourself and your Venusian Teacher.

By becoming more harmonious, loving, and aware, they will appear to you physically and in dreams. At first, you will receive revelations and helpful messages from your Teacher during your nightly dreams. However, these dreams will not be like your ordinary dreams. They will be extraordinarily vivid and intense, and impress you profoundly.

Whether or not you have seen your Venusian Teacher, the fact remains that he or she does exist, and is as real as you are. The Venusians are actual living entitles in masterful human form, and they have been helping Earthlings for countless centuries.

Contact will be made when your soul and its powers have reached the proper state. Do not seek to rush this, for it cannot be rushed. Banish the tendency to impatience, and like the rose, your soul shall unfold in great beauty.

Be ready, at all times, to obey whatever prompting

you may receive from us. Keep your faith firm, and by this attitude of communion and trust, you will be able to enter into communication with us.

Valiant Thor as he appeared in 1957, while speaking at Howard Menger's farm in New Jersey.

Printed in Great Britain
by Amazon

83621927R00037